MAY - - 2009

 W9-BBC-566

DISCARD

CHICAGO PUBLIC LIBRARY
BEVERLY BRANCH
1962 W. 95th STREET
CHICAGO, ILLINOIS 60643

CHICAGO, ILLINOIS 60601

THE BLACKFOOT

A TRUE BOOK®

by
Christin Ditchfield

CHICAGO PUBLIC LIBRARY
BEVERLY BRANCH
1962 W 95TH STREET
CHICAGO, IL 60643

Children's Press®
A Division of Scholastic Inc.

New York Toronto London Auckland Sydney
Mexico City New Delhi Hong Kong
Danbury, Connecticut

A Blackfoot tepee

Content Consultant
Liz Sonneborn

*The photograph on the title
page shows a Blackfoot girl.*

Library of Congress Cataloging-in-Publication Data
Ditchfield, Christin.
    The Blackfoot / by Christin Ditchfield.
        p. cm. — (A true book)
    Includes bibliographical references and index.
    0-516-23643-1 (lib. bdg.)   0-516-25587-8 (pbk.)
    1. Siksika Indians—Social life and customs—Juvenile literature.
2. Siksika Indians—History—Juvenile literature. I. Title. II. Series.
E99.S54D58 2005
978.004'97352—dc22   2004030519

© 2005 by Scholastic Inc.
All rights reserved. Published simultaneously in Canada.
Printed in the United States of America.

CHILDREN'S PRESS, and A TRUE BOOK™, and associated logos are
trademarks and/or registered trademarks of Scholastic Library Publishing.
SCHOLASTIC and associated logos are trademarks and/or registered
trademarks of Scholastic Inc.

1 2 3 4 5 6 7 8 9 10 R 14 13 12 11 10 09 08 07 06 05

R0429995365

Contents

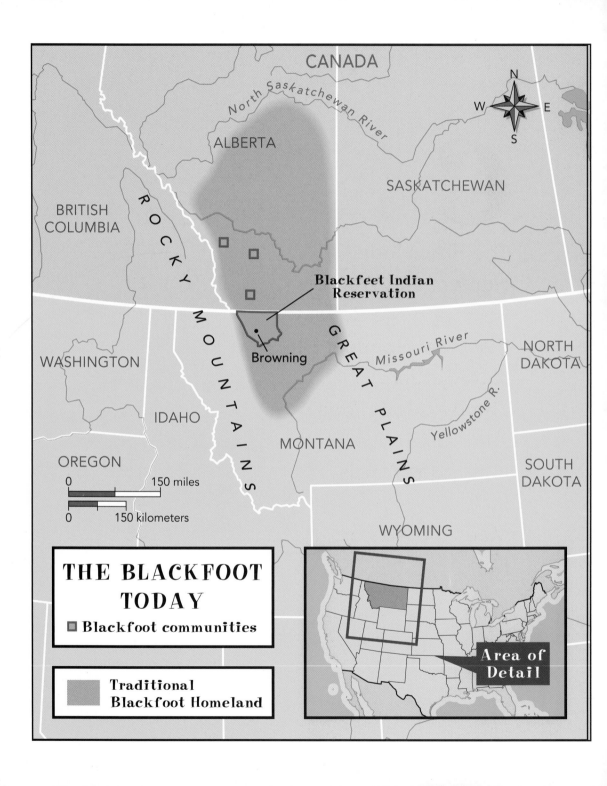

CANADA

North Saskatchewan River

ALBERTA

SASKATCHEWAN

BRITISH
COLUMBIA

R
O
C
K
Y

Blackfeet Indian
Reservation

M
O
U
N
T
A
I
N
S

Browning

G
R
E
A
T

Missouri River

NORTH
DAKOTA

WASHINGTON

P
L
A
I
N
S

Yellowstone R.

IDAHO

MONTANA

SOUTH
DAKOTA

OREGON

0   150 miles

0   150 kilometers

WYOMING

THE BLACKFOOT TODAY

◼ Blackfoot communities

Traditional
Blackfoot Homeland

Area of
Detail

The Plains Indians

American Indians have lived on the continent of North America for thousands of years. Many of these Algonquian people lived near the Great Lakes. They settled in parts of the present-day states of Minnesota, North Dakota, Michigan, and Canada. They raised their families and farmed the land.

Over time, the Algonquian people began to move away from the Great Lakes. They separated into different tribes. Each tribe developed its own distinct **culture** and language. By the 1600s, these tribes had become "people of the plains." Instead of living in one place, they traveled across the Great Plains, throughout the midwestern United States, and north into Canada. They moved from place to place in search of food,

Today, the Blackfoot live on a reservation in Montana just east of Glacier National Park (above).

following the herds to hunt and seeking good weather.

One of these tribes became known as the *Siksika*. This name probably comes from the Crow

7

Indian word meaning "black foot" or "black feet." The soles of their soft shoes were always black. No one knows for sure if the Siksika painted them that color or if it came from walking across the ashes of burned-out prairie fires.

The Blackfoot tribe was actually made up of four closely related tribes: the Northern Blackfoot (Siksika), the Bloods (*Kainah*), the Poorly Dressed or Piegans (*Pikuni*), and the Blackfoot.

The Piegans are one of the four closely related tribes that are known as the Blackfoot. Here a group of Piegan chiefs poses for a picture.

At one time, the Blackfoot controlled more **territory** than any other Great Plains tribe. They ranged from the North

The Blackfoot lived on the rolling hills and plains that border the Rocky Mountains to the east.

Saskatchewan River in Alberta, Canada, to the Upper Missouri River in Montana, southeast into North Dakota, and west to the base of the Rocky Mountains. They became skilled hunters and powerful warriors.

Hunters and Warriors

The Blackfoot traveled the Great Plains in bands of twenty or thirty, just the right number for a buffalo hunting party. In some places, the whole tribe—men, women, and children—would surround a herd of buffalo to keep them from stampeding. Then the hunters

A group of Blackfoot hunt buffalo on horseback.

would kill the buffalo one by one, using bows and arrows, lances, or spears. In other places, the hunters would chase or drive the buffalo over the edge of a cliff. The hunters then raced down to the bottom of the cliff to collect the dead and dying animals.

In the 1740s, the Blackfoot first obtained guns and horses. They may have gotten them from white traders or from other Indian tribes. The Blackfoot

The Blackfoot first obtained horses in the 1740s and soon became skilled horsemen.

quickly became expert horse-men. Horses made it much easier to herd and hunt buffalo.

The Blackfoot often used guns in raids on their enemies. These powerful warriors constantly fought other tribes. Sometimes they were defending their territory. More often, they were capturing horses— they could never have too many. The most skilled hunters and warriors became the wealthiest members of the tribe. They served as its chiefs or leaders.

Man's Best Friend

Before the Spanish explorers brought horses to North America, the Great Plains tribes depended on dogs to help them transport their belongings from place to place. The dogs pulled a travois, a kind of cart made from two long poles connected by a frame, that carried supplies. The dogs were also skilled

hunters, helping to herd buffalo and other game. They also stayed at the camp and protected the women and children when the men went off to battle. The Blackfoot treasured these precious animals.

Following the Buffalo

The Blackfoot followed the herds of buffalo across the Great Plains. They camped in cone-shaped tents called tepees. These tents were made of buffalo skins stretched over long wooden poles. When the tribe needed to move on, tepees could be taken down

17

A Blackfoot chief records his life story on the buffalo skins that form the walls of his tepee.

and later set up quickly and easily. Paintings of great warriors and hunters often decorated the walls of the tepees. The Blackfoot had very little furniture inside their homes. They slept on beds of buffalo robes and kept a fire burning for warmth.

The Blackfoot usually ate buffalo meat, although the men also hunted for mountain sheep, deer, and elk. When there was more buffalo meat than the group could eat right away, the women dried it and then pounded it into a kind of paste. They mixed the paste with buffalo fat, dried fruit, and seeds. This pemmican, or

Pemmican was an important food because it could be stored for a long time without spoiling.

jerky, was easy to carry from place to place. It could be stored for long periods of time. Pemmican came in handy, especially during winter when food was hard to find. Other foods included roots,

The women of the tribe gathered foods such as roots and berries to be used in soups and stews.

berries, and herbs. These were gathered by the women of the tribe and used to make soups and stews.

Chief Peh-to-pe-kiss, or Eagle's Ribs, wears clothing made of animal skins.

The Blackfoot made their clothing from animal skins, usually antelope, deer, or elk. Men wore shirts and leggings, along with breechcloths (aprons with front and back flaps hanging from the waist). Their head-dresses, or warbonnets, were different from those of other tribes. The feathers stood straight up in a crown shape, instead of fanning down and back. Women wore leggings and ankle-length sleeveless dresses decorated with paint, porcupine quills, and fringe. In cold weather, they attached long sleeves. Both men and

Some Blackfoot headdresses were different from those worn by the people of other tribes. The two men on the right wear typical Blackfoot head-dresses with feathers that stick straight up in the shape of a crown.

women wore soft animal skin shoes called moccasins. In the winter, they wore buffalo skin robes to keep warm.

The Blackfoot were skilled craftspeople. They designed and created many kinds of clothing, riding equipment, tools, and weapons. As they gained skill in hunting and battle, young men entered military societies. These were organized groups or clubs within the tribe, with names such as the Kit Foxes, Bulls, Horns, Braves, Crazy Dogs, and Little Birds. Brave and intelligent Blackfoot women had a society of their own, the *Motoki*.

Blackfoot Spiritual Life

The Blackfoot had a deep faith in the Creator God who made them and everything in the natural world. They believed that honoring the Creator would bring them health and happiness.

Each year, the tribe gathered for the Sun Dance, their most important religious ceremony.

An American Indian painting shows people participating in the Sun Dance. Many tribes had their own versions of the Sun Dance.

To prepare for the Sun Dance, members often went without food or sleep for days. Then they sang and danced and performed complex **rituals**. They smoked tobacco in a special

Pipes such as these were used to smoke tobacco. The pouch was used to hold tobacco.

medicine pipe. Those who were sick or injured presented offerings to the Creator as they prayed for healing. Young warriors participated in painful tests to prove their strength and **endurance**.

The Blackfoot often looked for spiritual guidance through visions and dreams. A young man would go out alone on a vision quest to hear what the Creator might say to him. Tribal members kept their own medicine bundles—rawhide pouches filled with personal belongings and **sacred** objects that were thought to have **supernatural** powers.

There were also medicine bundles that belonged to the whole tribe. To the Blackfoot, the beaver medicine bundle was the most powerful and sacred object of all. Tribal leaders used the objects in this bundle to assist them in planting tobacco for the medicine pipe. They believed that the beaver medicine bundle would bring them success in their buffalo hunts.

You Can Count to Ten in Blackfoot!

Nii-To-Ks-Ska	One	Na-Nii-Tso	Eight
Na-To-Ka	Two	Pih-Kso	Nine
Nii-Yo-Ks-Ska	Three	Kii-Poo	Ten
Nii-Tsoo-Woo	Four		
Nii-Tsi-To	Five		
Noi	Six		
Ih-Kii-Tsi-Ka	Seven		

New Settlers

In the early 1800s, President Thomas Jefferson asked a group of explorers to scout the land west of the Mississippi River. He sent them to see if they could find their way to the Pacific Ocean. When they returned, Americans heard their stories about the wonders of the West.

A pioneer family and their home

Soon thousands of white **settlers** began traveling across the Great Plains. Some claimed land, built homes, and began farming right in the middle of Blackfoot territory. Others just

A group of Blackfoot cross a river in Canada. Some members of the tribe moved north into Canada when white settlers began taking over their land.

passed through the area, seeking their fortunes farther west. Unfortunately, the land could not support all these people. The settlers' wagon trains disrupted the migrating patterns of the buffalo. Food became hard to find. The Blackfoot lands were never the same again.

The Blackfoot had to compete with other tribes for what was left of the land and its resources. Some bands moved farther north, into Canada. They hoped to avoid conflict with the white settlers. Other bands tried to protect their territory. They fought back against the U.S. army. These battles claimed the lives of hundreds of innocent men, women, and children.

As time went on, the Blackfoot lost many members of the tribe to war, starvation, and disease. They could not go on living as they had in the past. Blackfoot leaders signed peace treaties and agreed to move their people onto **reservations**. The Northern Blackfoot, Bloods, and Piegans settled on reserves, or reservations, in Alberta, Canada. The Blackfoot settled on a reservation in Montana.

The Blackfoot Today

Today, more than 37,000 people identify themselves as Blackfoot or Blackfeet. More than 15,000 Blackfoot still live on the reserves in Alberta, while about 8,000 live on the Blackfoot Reservation in Montana.

In many ways, the Blackfoot live like most other North Americans.

A Blackfoot man in traditional dress stands with a boy in a t-shirt.

They wear the same kinds of clothes and drive the same kinds of cars. They live in houses and apartment buildings. They

38

operate farms and lumber mills, breed cattle, and run businesses. In 1921, oil was discovered on the Montana reservation. Tribal members produce and sell more than 50 million barrels of oil each year.

Hundreds of thousands of tourists travel across the reservation on their way to visit Glacier National Park. Others come to hunt wildlife in the forests or fish in the many streams and lakes.

The Blackfoot work hard to preserve their history and keep their culture alive. They want to pass on their traditions to the next generation. Programs have been created to help children learn the language of their **ancestors**. Web sites and online groups help members of the tribe stay in touch. The Museum of the Plains Indians in Browning, Montana, honors their heritage with photographs and displays of Plains Indian life.

Many Blackfoot and other American Indians gather each summer at the North American Indian Days Celebration in Browning, Montana.

Each summer, the Blackfoot and other tribes from all over the Plains gather. They come to enjoy the North American Indian Days Celebration and

Young Blackfoot women celebrate their heritage by performing at a festival.

the Heart Butte Indian Days Festival. At these events, tribal members dress in traditional costumes. They sing and dance and play the drums. They share arts and crafts and recipes. Members play games, compete in rodeos, and march in parades. They celebrate their rich heritage with one another and with other Americans. It is a time to show the world how wonderful it is to be a Blackfoot!

To Find Out More

Here are some additional resources to help you learn more about the Blackfoot:

 **Books**

Gibson, K. **Blackfeet: People of the Dark Moccasins.** Capstone Press, 2003.

Gray, Barbara A. **Blackfoot.** ABDO Publishing Company, 2002.

Hendrickson, Ann-Marie. **Blackfeet Indians.** Chelsea House Publishers, 1997.

Kavasch, E. Barrie. **Blackfoot Children and Elders Talk Together.** The Rosen Publishing Group, 1999.

Ryan, Marla Felkins, and Linda Schmittroth. **Blackfoot.** Gale Group, 2002.

⚙ Organizations and Online Sites

Blackfeet Creation Tale
http://www.montana.edu/wwwbcc/legend.html

Read the story of how Old Man created people and taught them how to survive in the world.

The Blackfeet Nation
P.O. Box 850
Browning, MT 59417
www.blackfeetnation.com

Visit this site to learn more about Blackfoot history and culture. Discover the Blackfoot firefighting group known as the Chief Mountain Hotshots and learn more about tribal government and activities.

National Museum of the American Indian
Fourth Street and Independence Avenue SW
Washington, DC 20024
202-633-1000
http://www.nmai.si.edu/

Visit the museum to learn more about American Indian history and culture.

U.S. Department of the Interior Indian Arts and Crafts Board
http://www.doi.gov/iacb/museum/museum_plains.html

Visit this site to learn more about the Museum of the Plains Indian in Browning, Montana.

Important Words

ancestor member of a person's family who lived long ago

culture the way of life of a group of people

endurance ability to last for a long time

reservation land set aside by the government as a place for American Indians to live (known as reserves in Canada)

ritual a set of actions always performed in the same way

sacred holy; having to do with religion; something deserving of great respect

settler a person who makes a home in a new place

supernatural something that science and natural law cannot explain

territory a large area of land belonging to a particular group or government

Index

Meet the Author

Christin Ditchfield is an author, conference speaker, and host of the nationally syndicated radio program *Take It to Heart!* Her articles have been featured in magazines all over the world. A former elementary school teacher, Christin has written more than thirty books for children on a wide range of topics, including sports, science, and history. She makes her home in Sarasota, Florida.

Photographs © 2005: Art Resource, NY/Smithsonian American Art Museum, Washington, DC, USA: 22; Bridgeman Art Library International Ltd., London/New York: 33 (Archives Charmet), 14 (The Stapleton Collection); Corbis Images: 27 (Werner Forman), 41 (Steve Kaufman), 18 (Underwood & Underwood), 9; Getty Images/Hulton Archive/MPI: 16; Mary Evans Picture Library: 34; National Anthropological Archives, Smithsonian Institution, Washington, DC: 24; Nativestock.com/Marilynn "Angel" Wynn: cover, 1, 2, 20, 21, 28, 31, 38, 43; Raymond Bial: 10; Stock Montage, Inc.: 12; The Image Works/Sonda Dawes: 7.
Map by Bob Italiano: 4.